Cheddar Grits

Chantel Miller

FIRST EDITION

ISBN: 9781097882052

For my mother.

Thank you, my love. You are the vertebrae to my spine and I appreciate every ounce of support that you have poured into my being. Since childhood, you have instilled in me the importance of being exactly who I am and supported every step I have taken since the first one. You deserve the world and then some and I will always give it my all. There isn't a word in the dictionary to describe how much I love you. I looked for one.

For my father.

Thank you for seeing me and lifting me up when sometimes I wasn't sure which way up was. Thank you for showing me that it isn't too late to love hard and love with my all. Most importantly, thank you for being there when I wasn't always the best at letting others be there for me. You are kind and your heart is special. I love you.

For my family.

You all have been a girl's dream cheering section. My family is not huge but it is warm and inviting. You all make 50 sound like 5,000 and you all have no idea how much that has impacted me throughout life. Support systems are everything and I am blessed to have a divine one.

For my friends.

You all are the family that I was fortunate enough to create over the years. Thank you for attending every poetry show and snapping your fingers off. Thank you for encouraging me to express myself despite my insecurities. I am so thankful to have had you all in my life and to have met you at the exact moments that I did. I love each and every one of you.

CONTENTS

AUTHOR'S NOTE

If you have ever taken a trip to the southern United States, there is a good chance you have been introduced to a savory bowl of cheddar grits. Grits in itself is a rather simple and almost humble food. Though it may appear to be plain, it is actually a whole grain offered in various ways. This simplistic yet nutritious food can be the base of breakfast, lunch, dinner, and sometimes even dessert. It's all in the way you prepare it.

Just recently, I discovered that my favorite dish could be brought back to life after once thinking that once it became cold and congealed, it was of no real use. Some folks like to repurpose theirs and that's fine. I'm more of a nice, warm, creamy, savory, grit person myself. Imagine my delight when I slowly but surely warmed some cheddar grits back to their original and creamy glory the next day.

As I stirred the pot, I realized that this was nothing more than a metaphor for life. We get ground down throughout the years and we often have to figure out what we can do with the pieces that once made us whole; we have to figure out how to present ourselves over and over in a presentable and palatable way. Like grits, we can come together and become something that is flexible and applicable in a number of situations. We can add spices and cream and butter for flavor. We can be presented warmly or we can become cold and congealed. It is then that we must decide if life has ground us down enough that we can no longer find our original form or if we would rather be repurposed into something better.

This batch of cheddar grits that I have whipped up for you all is more than an anthology. It is a non-sequential poetic memoir and compilation of short stories reflecting my life up until this point. It is my hope that I have created something warm and hearty for your minds as I have spent countless hours prepping my soul to be shared.

With that being said, how do you like your grits?

Cheddar Grits

RAW

Hello

Allow me to introduce some facts about me.
I love cherry jolly ranchers...
or cherry anything.
I purposely pick all the cherry candies out...sorry.
My favorite color is yellow.
I am writer, an artist, and the occasional
photographer.
I've got the eye.
I spend more time in my thoughts than I should.
I fall viciously in love with people I find fascinating.
I keep it cool and never show my emotions if I can
help it.
No sweat, baby.
I analyze people for a while before I ever even speak
to them.
I'm not affectionate but when I am, get ready for the
LOVE.
I'm a little shameless.
I am talented and often question why I have been
given so many gifts, but I am grateful for them.
When people compliment me, I never believe them
but I always say 'thank you.'
I believe that my friends were God sent as my
protectors because I don't know where I'd be without
them.
I have an extreme fear of failure in regards to a lot of
things.
Sometimes I'm too blunt.
Sometimes I'm too indirect.
I love cold weather and soup.

I don't smile often, but I joke a lot as to take the attention off of me.
When I do smile...it is genuine.
My name is Chantel...and I'm an optimistic pessimist.

My Tumultuous Relationship with Poetry

I don't write when I'm happy—
or in love.
I say that like love comes my way often,
like I trust these reckless beings with something as
vital as my heart.
No trust issues—
just that people define love differently than I do.
I only write when I'm broken.
It's the only time that metaphors make sense to me—
when the world is collapsing
or maybe I'm falling into something I know will be
the death of me
emotionally.
What people don't understand is that
I'm not a fan of poetry.
It's actually a consequence of my sensitivity
and the only thing that understands the hurt when
it's time.
I guess I used her—[poetry]
because when the words come out,
everyone loves how beautiful you made the pain
sound.
Whatever the case,
I'm having a hard time writing this.
Poetry knows I never really settle down for longer
than a little while.
I'll be back when the happiness is gone...
because just like me,
it never stays long.

Mahogany's Kiss Backstory

When I wrote this, it was a painful time in our country. Trayvon Martin had just been slain and though our country had been through this type of thing several times over, it seemed to affect us all more potently. There was something about seeing the footage of a young man just innocently purchasing some items from a convenience store, only to be murdered moments later. That truly struck me as it did so many others. Hailing from the south myself, I know all too well what it feels like to look racism directly in the face and not be able to say anything because I love my life just enough not to. It still hurts when someone is taken away so abruptly. It still hurts when they look like me.

Mahogany's Kiss

Before I was born
my skin was kissed by Mahogany.
And as I got older
I began to see it as a blessing
that my skin was unique
and such a beautiful part of me.
I loved how my father's chocolate complexion
combined with my mother's caramel tone
and was a reflection of me —

Mahogany.

But to learn that not all of society would feel the
same was unbelievable.
To have to accept that the color of my skin could
make me worthy of mistreatment
was inconceivable.
A product of the South,
I didn't understand why the color of my skin
being darker than my Caucasian friends was such a
problem.

Racism.

Race is just a word that is applied to group of people
to distinguish them from another.
It's based solely on physical characteristics.
In other words,
we're all biologically the same,
but because my skin is darker
some feel the need to call me out of my name.

And why do they keep telling me to go back to
where I came from?

If I go…

Wouldn't they have to go too?
This land…doesn't belong to *them.*
And if it wasn't for people like them,
I wouldn't even be here.
Bringing my ancestors here,
claiming this land as their own,
calling it home,
Bold.

But…I don't blame *them* for that.
And I try to leave those bitter feelings in the past
because I think it's kind of sad
to get so mad over things I didn't actually
experience.
But America makes it hard when they treat those
with Mahogany skin
like bulletproof experiments.

Eradicate the Black man.

He doesn't belong on this land.
Blue uniforms get tough with a piece of steel.
It seems like they get a thrill
when they're forcing one of color down to the
ground against his will.

Don't move [nigga]. You better not move, [nigga].
You have the right to remain silent.

How are we to remain quiet when our lives are at
stake?
Begging for your own life because you've been
kissed by Mahogany is a risk you have to take —
if you're given the chance.
But more than likely
those words will never be heard.

Most of them never even had a chance to look
around before guns fired 50 rounds —
one shot to the back,
one shot to the chest,
or even a lethal dosage to inject.
Take your pick.

Because if Black isn't going back to where it came
from
then Black isn't coming back alive.
Ask blue uniforms why they did it
and they'll say something callous
like they felt threatened by an unarmed man whose
life ended
in a matter of minutes.
And just about every one of them gets acquitted.

Injustice.

When you see me,
do you feel threatened by my brown skin?
Do you automatically assume that I want to harm
you?
That I'm loud and obnoxious and that I apply *by any
means necessary* to my daily routine?
Do you think I'm mean?

On my way to class,
Do you feel that your life is in jeopardy when I pass?
Surely there's some sort of weapon in my backpack
right?
I guess books about Psychology,
Anthropology,
and mythology could be seen as a real danger in
your eyes.

We were desegregated to come together and truly be
united,
but instead…we're still divided.
Yet on a piano,
Ebony and ivory can make such beautiful harmony
but not with people it seems.

Self-defense is not one man who is unarmed getting
shot in his back.
Self-defense is not three unaware men have 50
bullets rain down on them.
Self-defense is a not a seventeen year old taking his
last breath because one man found him suspicious
and put a bullet in his chest.

When I was kissed by Mahogany,
I didn't understand that justice wasn't meant for me
or that it was only meant for those coated in cream
that my skin was not one of those that society would
accept…
or protect.
I didn't understand that being kissed by Mahogany
meant not being able to be proud of myself.

There's no time to be proud because the cries of my
people are just way too loud
to ignore.

I never knew
that all this would come from Mahogany's Kiss.

Wishful Thinking

There are times when I wish we'd never met,
never crossed paths,
because all these fantasies are just in my mind.
They keep me up at night,
from thinking straight during the day...
because I know someone as incredible as you is just
walking around
gracing the lives of others.

I'm selfish.

I want you to grace me with your presence
and I want to become overly intoxicated because I
had a little too much of your rich goodness.
I already over indulge in your mere existence.
I wonder if you've ever experienced an altruistic love
such as mine?
You'll never understand how quickly I float to the
skies when you say hello,
how I melt in the heartiness of your laugh,
or how quickly I fall from the clouds when I hear the
sadness in your goodbye.

It's never goodbye....

It's see you later,
just to save ourselves some heartache.
Occasionally I reminisce about our first few
conversations,

how we bypassed getting to know one another
because it felt like we'd known each other a few
lifetimes.
Have you any idea how good it feels to interact with
someone you've known all your life,
In every life?

Oh I forgot,
this is all in my head.

My Bad

No, I shouldn't have done it.
I shouldn't have opened the door to your heart
when I wasn't ready...
My hands weren't clean enough to massage
insecurities from trust issue laden arteries.
I kept retreating into my own comfort zone
bouncing in whenever I so pleased,
always forgetting to wipe my feet on the doormat
that clearly said
"caution"
instead of
"welcome."
Too often
I left carbon footprints in your chambers.
I've been too reckless with your unconditional,
lost my keys to your love and tried to pick my way
in.

I'm sorry for breaking the locks the last time.

You wouldn't believe me if I said this time I'll stay —
so just know I gave up the keys to my comfort zone.

It really wasn't all the comfortable anymore
anyway.

Apprehensions

Scared.

I'm terrified of being in your presence
even if only for a little while.
I fear that I'll miss you too much when the time
comes for me to go
or you to go...
and let's face it,
there's nothing worse than a goodbye kiss
except the opportunity that goes missed
when there is no chance to have it.
So this is a bit of a contradiction.

Hear me out.

I do want to see you,
I really do,
I just don't want to miss you.
That's the problem,
I want to be with you all the time.
There isn't a day that goes by that I don't think about
us,
not me alone and you alone trying to make a distant
us.
I'm thinking about us
together.
Take that however you please,
'cause I want to please you all the time,
whether that be physically,
mentally,
or emotionally.

13

I'd like to personally be able to give you things just
for the hell of it—
kiss you on your forehead and tell you it's going to
be okay
when you're having a bad day.
I just want to be there
or have you here.
It doesn't matter as long you're near me.

I don't want to miss you.

Look at all the things I have to miss out on while
missing you.
I don't want to miss the feel of you.
Please,
imprint yourself on my arms so they may never
know the goodness of an embrace unless it's yours.
Allow my hands time to memorize how you feel for
the days when I can't touch you,
but I can always feel you.
Understand that I'm not staring at you when I'm
close,
I'm just tattooing every inch of you on my brain for
the time we must spend apart.
I'll probably take something small from you when
you aren't looking,
something you won't notice is gone just for a
keepsake,
and hopefully it'll have your scent on it—
So I can inhale you deep into my lungs and for a
minute,
I'll be closer to you than I could ever wish to be until
the next time.
I just need you to understand…

I don't want to have to miss you.
It scares me.

Supercell

I imagine that sometimes,
my heart doesn't beat so subtly,
that it's contractions sound more like the thunderous
claps of a summer storm.
While the veins that envelop my body
are merely lightening bolts absorbing the shock of
how life's embrace
can leave me so seemingly calm,
while conjuring up a natural disaster beneath the
surface.
All too often I am left feeling like a contradiction
just as ice chunks find a way to fall from hot skies.
My daily routine leaves my insides twisted up,
wrenched in a whirlwind of emotions.
It always takes longer than I care to spend rebuilding
myself after the corruption is over.

I guess my fear of thunderstorms doesn't seem so
irrational now.

Letter To My Ex Backstory

To sum this poem up in a nutshell, I was hurt. I like to say that we all become artists when we experience pain. At the time, I had never felt such a pain in my life. When this happened, you couldn't tell me that someone wasn't ripping my heart out of my chest and using it as a cutting board. Though I had written a few things here and there in my life, this was the first time I had ever written a full blown poem that cohesively came together to express how I felt. Metaphors came naturally and I felt like I was purging my emotions as best I knew how at the precious age of nineteen. First loves and first breakups make you feel everything on a level you never knew existed simply because they are the firsts. The most important lesson I took from this is that first should be the implication that it won't be the last by any means.

Letter To My Ex

I loved you.
Better yet
that's the past tense.
I love you.
I won't deny that it still exists.
As an artist,
if I tried to paint it,
there wasn't enough paint in the world to artistically
recreate the amount of love in me.
My pencils couldn't sketch anything so beautiful
and my hands could never mold clay into anything
so wonderful.
As a poet,
my mind just couldn't come up with enough poetic
rhymes
to justify
how much I love you.
But as a photographer,
my camera wasn't quick enough and failed to
capture my heart breaking because of you.
And you didn't care.
Come my way again?
You wouldn't dare.
Most would think the way I treated you was unfair,
but never that.
I placed you on a pedestal higher than the rest
and I may not consider myself one of the better
but I gave you my very best.

I was there for you.

When no one else really cared
and your life was falling apart
and nothing going as planned,
I was there.
Pulled you out of the dirt and brushed you off,
held you close and told you I'd never run off.
Dedicated not only myself and my mind
but my heart
and all of my time to you.

Whatever you wanted
you had it.
Never had to ask,
it was automatic.
Love.
I had never let myself experience anything so great
before you.
I allowed myself to participate
in this destined fate
and I shouldn't have.
I can't regret something that was once so beautiful
but to let myself get hurt like this
was beyond crucial.
Pain like that should not be legal
yet the words that pass your lips are far worse
and somewhat lethal.

What did I ever do for you to hate me?

I don't want to seem like I'm dwelling on memories
in photos past
but there's a huge chunk of film that never reached
exposure.
Please,

all I need is some closure.

What did I do?

Loved you with every fiber of my natural being...
was I not supposed to?
Is there something I'm just not seeing?
Maybe I'm just oblivious.
Because you told me that you loved me with all of
your heart
that I was amazing and we'd never grow apart.
I should have known that this would be trouble from
the start
that I love you is just a phrase when exchanged from
you to me.
There were no feelings behind it
and it was all just a game in reality
or
maybe it wasn't.

I don't know.

Honestly,
You left me without any good reasons
and the few you gave were all reasons someone
would want to stay.
So tell me why you left that way?

Confusion drives me partially insane.
Tears form whenever I hear your name.
I can't take it.
To this day,
my heart literally aches
and I can feel the dull throbbing deep in my chest

but I'm staying away because that's what you want
and you say it's best.
But I really can't handle this.

Those others are only concerned with loving your
body and face
succumbing to the pleasures only as deep as the skin.

I just wanted to touch your heart.

Something true and from deep within.
I mean,
does it bother you that I can peer into the depths of
your soul
looking past the skin
chiseling away at the stone around your heart
and making it to the center where our love could
grow?
Does it bother you?

Maybe you never thought I would make it that close.
Maybe you loved me a little too much
and it scared you to know that I was real
that you could have the ability to feel something so
surreal.
Or not.
Tell me because I don't know.

I took a chance for you,
falling victim to my own desires,
stepped out onto that wire
and walked the tightrope of love for you.
I thought you were walking this thin line with me

but all along you had a knife slowly cutting the other end
and right before I could reach you,
it was then and only then that you let me fall
mercilessly in love with you.

Only for me to hit the hard concrete of actuality
falling deeper than the depths of my mentality
and there was no netting to catch me.
My body broke into a million pieces
and my heart splattered upon the earth
waiting for you to come seize it and mend it back to health again.
But instead,
you stomped on it and smeared it back into the earth
as if giving it back to me would be more trouble than its worth.

How could I have misread you?
You handled my heart so carelessly,
peeled a few pieces from the ground,
tossed them in a box and tossed it my way with a smile as if to say,
"Here, I don't want it anymore."

You could have at least given my all the pieces of my broken heart back.

I'm not going to seek vengeance because I'll let karma handle that.
This game that you call love makes me push others away,
yet the possibility of loving another is beautiful...
someday.

I just don't understand how we went from lovers and
best friends
to enemies who can't even speak unless arguing until
the conversation ends.
These feelings are getting the best of me,
killing me slowly.
Please,
Just let this be over…
but I love you.

Sometimes I wish that I could forget you
but the possibility of having to live without you
seems like an impossible reality to live with.

How much does it take to explain that this
hurts a little bit more than heartache?
And somehow,
through all this,
You're still perfect in my eyes.
I'm done.
I'll just let this be
goodbye.

COOKED

A Love Like

I heard a love story.
Not your run of the mill
fantasy where everything is all perfect story.
There was sadness,
confusion,
miscommunication,
and heartbreak.
It was painfully beautiful,
how after 60 years of separation...
love still found its way home.
It reassured me that I wasn't insane,
that the way I feel for you may never die.
I know I have always loved you recklessly;
how cautious would it be for me to pretend this heart
doesn't beat for you?
So...I could have faith in coincidence
but,
I can't possibly let half a century go by without
properly loving you.

Peace Love

I love you calmly.

It used to bother me,
how my stomach never felt the flutter of butterflies,
that my heart never raced at the sound of your voice,
how my mind forgot to panic at your smile.

Then I realized...
I love you calmly.

Smooth like the tide,
we flow over one another,
melt into each other's being.
Wrap me in your solitude.
Hold me in your peace.

I love you calmly.

Unconditionally,
as a mother loves her unborn child.
It's constant and true,
unyielding as she nurtures what she cannot
physically hold
or see.
This is you for me.

I love you calmly.

And I will never regret that.

PRNDL

Park the car...
leave it running because it's too hot not to.
It's dark but we never needed light to feel one
another.
Words caress skin just as effectively as fingers do.
Tell me your dreams and ambitions,
your fears and inhibitions.
I'll tell you that the only thing I'm actually afraid of is
myself.
How self-sabotage has been my worst enemy since
anxiety moved in,
settled next door to my dreams.
Lean the seats all the way back,
stare at the textures in the fabric and imagine the
moon
until we can afford a moon roof ironically just to see
the stars
In this parked car.
We laugh because at least we aren't as broke as we
were in college,
and student loans aren't the worst in exchange for a
little knowledge...
We grimace because we could have gotten this
education cheaper somewhere else,
explored the world and been a little more cultured,
acquired more depth...
But hey, we're doing our best.
Reverse.
Back up to when we first met,
swift encounter,
Both socially awkward and didn't say anything,

but I saw you...
I noticed you.
I can't forget you.
Shifted to drive,
maybe even overdrive getting to know one another.
Lost in the similarities and weaving through the
stand still awkward moments when neither of us
knew what to say,
but we kept moving forward,
when maybe we should have been patient enough to
enjoy the moment—
take in the scenery.
Running out of gas even though my tank was full,
I was starting to feel empty.
Did we fizzle out?
Rode too much now you need a break,
but not entirely.
Just coast in neutral for a while,
Slowed to a stop
Drifted all the way apart...
Life happens, I guess.
No real explanation,
life just had different routes for us,
Separate cars and separate journeys,
different speeds in different directions but still
somehow crossing one another's path just enough...
to miss one another.
I've had enough.
Stop driving aimlessly in circles and pick you up so
we can find a destination together.
Switch to low gear because now we've got all this
baggage—
so much has happened
but I don't mind towing it all.

That's what we have to do to really connect
acknowledge all our imperfections and realize that
our personalities all have defects.
Nobody's perfect,
as long they're worth it...
So here we are again...
I put the car in park again...
Tell me,
what's new?

Prototype Backstory

I think it's fair to say that we all meet someone that possesses all the qualities we would want in a partner but it isn't always ideal to be with them. This poem is named after a song that I've always loved by OutKast by the same name. To me, it seems to be such a sweet gesture that someone could impact you so much that if you cannot have them, you hope to have someone like them. When I ran to an individual like this, I realized right away that the song played in my head. It was mesmerizing and I felt like I was floating most of the time but I'm also severely realistic. So one could only hope that this amazing person is the one, but if not, let's at least hope they're the prototype for the best to come along.

Prototype

Prototype.
The first.
The initial glimpse of a tangible product.
Tangible:
perceived by the ability to touch.
Because before it was nothing more than a concept,
a fantasy,
a dream.
I drew you in pastels and charcoal before I met you.
Crafted and sculpted you into something tangible,
but I failed to breathe life into you.
Because...you were unrealistic.
Impossible to exist in this fast paced world —
too perfect for mere mortals so I pushed you to the
back of mind.
Just left you there to dust over and be forgotten.
I needed to lower my standards.
My mind concocted something out of my league,
to be built by my clumsy yet gifted hands in hopes
that maybe this prototype would lead to the real
deal.
You were a dream far before you were a reality and
now...
here you stand,
motivating me to create again,
to write again,
to love...
again.
Artists don't create to see their work come to life,
but rather they thrive from the way spirits light up,

at how their crazy thoughts transformed into
something physical...
makes you feel something.
And you make me feel everything
because you were my creation,
full of broken bits of me,
tears from uneasy nights,
laughs for the good times,
smiles that seem convincing,
but I know better than that.
Your eyes smile at me just as your lips,
and I can't help but to stare dead into them,
feeling bolder than ever,
not afraid to be myself,
not tripping over my flaws
or shying away when my heart starts beating so
hard,
I fear my rib cage can't contain it.
And you used to scare me...
I never thought I'd be lucky enough to have my
dreams come true.
That you were a beautiful imaginary fantasy,
But good vibes don't just happen with everyone.
Hugs that make you feel whole could never take
place with a stranger.
You must have superpowers,
to make an emotionally paralyzed person feel again.
the warmth in your laughter,
the strength in your embrace,
the beauty in you simply being is breathtaking.
Oddly enough,
even though I crafted you so long ago,
I never programmed your heart to love me.

That's why you're my prototype.

"I hope that you're the one. If not, you are the prototype..."

Honeysuckle

I was once reminded of the light within me,
how the petals of a flower child
blossomed in my presence.
Not a hippie
but you're all about love and not so much peace.
The rebel of your domain.
Please show me how God created you to turn a blind
eye to insecurities
and focus solely on what made you feel good—
the rays of the sun,
the light of your world.
As long as I rise you are okay,
because you need me...
and I need you to need me.
Co-dependency,
that's how we survive
in a world full of enemies.
Like the hummingbird and honeysuckle,
I seek inspirational nourishment from your mind.

Knots

I want to get caught up in the knots of your soul
and give all new meaning to the feeling of butterflies
in the pit of your stomach.
You are the most complex jigsaw puzzle I've ever
seen
and I promise I'm not the type to flee at the sight of
difficulty.
I won't drop this project for something easier because
I look at you and see abstract elements obscurely
placed,
just trying to find a way to fit wherever they may.

Maybe I'm the one to help you figure it out and feel
normal again.

Black Carpets Backstory

Unfortunately, I got slammed with anxiety in my mid-twenties. It crept up on me and though I may have had some experience with it in the past unbeknownst to myself, the event that set it off completely hit me out of the blue. On that specific day, nothing had occurred when I had my very first panic attack. I was terrified and my body felt things that it had never felt before. I was medically evaluated and the doctors told me that I was most likely experiencing a panic attack.

This attack was so severe that it took several weeks for my nervous system to get back in order. I would have another before things began to balance out again. What's really sad about this is that when my doctor asked me what was going on, I simply replied "nothing." I didn't think there was anything out of the ordinary. She encouraged me to share what had been going on in my life because anxiety doesn't just come from nothing.

So I opened up. When I did, my doctor looked me dead in the eyes and said, "Oh no baby, you've been through more than most 25 year olds could dare to imagine. No wonder you're having panic attacks."

That was the day I started seeking help for what people of color tend to sweep under the rug.

Black Carpets

Picture it —

My apartment bedroom floor,
some random night around 3 am.
Existential crisis number seven hundred ninety
three…
and counting.
In the midst of tears and unwanted snot bubbles,
trying to figure out why normality seems so distant.
I remember my how much I hate carpet.
Random I know,
and it's not unclean,
I'm just somewhat the germaphobe.
My brain can't help but think of all the people who
have cycled through my bedroom before I ever knew
of its existence.

This is gross.

My mind wanders back to that stain in the living
room,
how I'm unsure as to what it is and why it never
went away,
even after I steam cleaned,
it came back.
I just really want to know…what is that?!

Over think.

You know,
someone could have died right there
and no one would say a thing.
My monthly rent is far more important than lives
lead by past tenants.

Whatever.

I start pulling myself together,
Realizing that carpet and people are somewhat alike.

Carpets…

Complex,
manmade,
woven fibers.
They hold on to things like stains and allergens.
No matter how often you vacuum,
after a while those lines just won't show anymore.
Worn down and frayed.
And rugs all the same.
They allow people to sweep their truths underneath
them.
And it would seem that my people have become
entirely too good at turning a blind eye.

Black might not crack,
but Black will stain.

You just can't see it as well.
We walk around just as broken as everyone else
with smiling faces,
Masters at disguising our pain
because it's best to let it all fall in God's hands in
anyway.
We are often discouraged from seeking professionals
trained to analyze our brains.
Call us crazy for paying so much money just talk
because it's much more affordable to pray.

But you can't see damage of a self-inflicted beat
down,
so people just assume all is okay.

Constantly under pressure,
trying to be better.
But not too good that we forget where we come from.

Conflicted.

Caught up in the whirlwind of trying to actually be
okay
and making sure everyone just thinks we're okay.

Never sure,
so we stop just long enough to hold our phones up,
smile and take a quick photo of the self.
Not convinced the self has any worth anymore until
someone else tells us it does.

Double Tap.

Daily validation from strangers seems more
important than balance
and last I checked,
the internet was the most dangerous place to seek
acceptance.
But we need it.
We really think we need it
because we've been programmed to check profiles
before checking on each other.
It's easier that way.

"I'm fine and you?" tends to pass our lips before we
have time to process the question.
People don't really want to know about the wine
stain daddy issues deeply rooted in our fibers.

It makes us look like damaged goods.

Since talking about how you feel in the Black
community is so taboo,
we ignore the fact that those same daddies probably
have daddy issues too.

Some of us are still scrubbing muddy footprints left
by family members too prideful to admit they felt
hopeless,
dragged us through the mud with them
and wiped their insecurities away on the welcome
mats of our individuality.

We don't really know who we are.

We simply reflect whatever has been swept under
our rugs,
the sneaky things left in our fibers that eventually
present themselves
no matter how much we clean house.
There will always be little clues
like the prescription drugs I used to use to stabilize
my mood.
They missed my mouth one time too many,
tired of feeling like a zombie.

I just really needed someone to listen.

But Black families always cliché that everything will
be alright too often.
And it just might.
But we can't keep blowing off mental health because
it can't be seen with the naked eye.

The church has been a wonderful Band-Aid
but for far too long.
Some of these wounds need stitches;
so many of us walking around critically injured.
Yet, we look good.

Scrub off the top layer but there's some grime left
deep at the roots.

Try to picture this:
Our minds are complex and woven like fibers.
They hold on to trauma and leave us stained.
And repressed memories?

Nothing more than allergens left behind,
that pop up and bother us from time to time.
Most of us are pretty good people.
We just rather not look so broken.

Black has been through too much to look weak now.

So we sweep our anxieties under our well-kept rugs
but eventually,
Black Carpets will be too worn down to hide
anything.

Look at us...
we're fraying.

COLD

Just Venting

They say,
getting over someone you never actually dated can
be harder than a breakup.
I agree.
It was an almost,
and almost is never good enough,
just close enough
to remind you that you weren't enough.
That's tough
realizing that someone could see all your worth
yet not find the value in it to stay.
All these games we play,
with each other's hearts.
Feel feelings deeper than depths we imagined.
Feel each other's souls smile when around each
other,
because this is how it's supposed to be.
Both been broken before...
But with each other we finally felt free.
And we both can feel something real,
something surreal,
What a thrill...
until it's not.
Rather push me away than let your guard down,
hurt me because you can't handle how you feel.
You know this is real.
This is us.
You and me.
We've been a team.
Labels we don't need.
The lines have been blurred for some time

and now you'd rather let me go than just be.
Tell me I can't handle how things have to be.
Maybe because it doesn't make sense to me?
Everything is very black and white,
Either you do or you don't,
I don't rest on in between.

They say...
getting over someone you never actually dated is
harder than a breakup.
I agree.
I'm not too prideful to admit that you played me,
To the best of your degree,
I'm mad,
I'm angry,
I'm upset that you could actually do this to me.
You're so subtle
and selfish with me.
Take up all my time then say I'm not someone you
need.

What was your point?

I can't read your mind.
My heart is tired of being kind and understanding.
Tell me how you really feel—
not how you think you should feel.
Tell me what you want—
not what you've always wanted.
Desires change and so do people.
So what if your love didn't come in the package you
always envisioned?
You'd rather pack it up and return to sender?

How long will you hold out for what you always wanted when you already had it?

They say...
getting over someone you never actually dated is harder than a break up.
I really...really...
agree.

Ice Sculpture

You left,
then told me I didn't fight for you
and since no one wanted to talk about it,
a cold shoulder just became an acceptable form of I
love you too.

We never acknowledged those feelings,
the ones that froze and shattered
well before hitting either of our eardrums.

How could we be so stubborn?

You Up?

I asked my mom the other night,
"What if Dad randomly texted you at 1 am just to
say, aye uhhh you up?"
She laughs.
I argue anything is possible.

My parents got divorced when I was 2,
which means that whole family unit thing is
something I never knew
but I've always known the meaning of family.

Although we found the humor in the possibility of
that text,
maybe an hour later,
in so many words,
I got that iconic...
"Hey um....you up?"
I'm bombarded with I love yous,
showered with soulmate promises,
visions of grandeur and all that other nonsense.
Followed by trying to figure out where I've been,
or how I've been MIA from a person who found no
problem ignoring me when I was all about them.
It was late and I was tired,
but not physically.
Just no energy left to go through the run around
again.
Here you go singing that song...
No this isn't another again
and there's nothing beautiful about not being able to
get this right.

51

You tell me you're just a terrible person
but you love me.
After the umpteenth time of hearing that
and giving up on whatever we had...
I interpret it more like you don't love me enough to
do better.
Just get it together.
I won't coddle your insecurities.
It finally makes sense to me...
how people get caught up in the cycle —
You know when they're just good enough that you
can't really say anything too bad,
but bad enough that there's never really anything
good to say...
anyway.
Something good that became damaged goods.
People like that are so insecure that they project their
brokenness onto you,
to the point that you actually start to question if
there's something wrong with you.
That's just how they do,
have you really questioning all that makes you...you.
And you start to lose it...
Because after a while you know the routine —
One or two Fridays out of the month at midnight it
seems,
they find themselves trying to figure out where they
went wrong with you.
But wait...
they play victim too.
So they'll tell you EXACTLY what's wrong with you,
picking at old scabs,
continuously telling you why it won't work
even though you never asked.

They say they just can't let you get that close again,
when the truth is they probably never let you in.
And it was never your fault,
I promise.
Just let them have a little pity party for themselves,
because it will always be woe is me and what could
have been.
Isn't it exhausting?
Being a broken mess?
Being in love but too afraid to commit?
Wanting to have something but knowing you're too
immature to actually have it?
Aren't you tired?
Because God knows I am.
When my phone lights up with song lyrics...
I wonder why you have to tell me through song.
Speaking from the heart isn't all that hard is it?
We've been doing this for way too long.
After nearly a decade,
The next time you hit me with all these feelings after
11 pm,
for the first time,
I won't be up.
You don't have control anymore.
And I know it's already eating you up.
See,
My parents got divorced when I was 2.
And though the family unit is something I never
knew,
I know it's nothing like this.
So, no I'm not up.
You should probably just get some rest.
I'm no longer a reason for you to be stressed.
Goodnight.

Tolerance

I'm tired of paying for your obsession
how you loved the thought of love
and became addicted to the routine.
You plundered through people
and hardened yourself along the way as a means
of protection.

What are you so afraid of?
Feeling again?
That you might beat the odds and fall in love again?
And then
what?

You push me away because I'm ideal.
Want me next to you but refuse to feel
and I force you to feel everything without trying.
You tell me you love me but can't stay.
You hold my heart close to yours but never let it rest.

I'm tired of tolerating this behavior;
of paying for your mistakes.
Tell me I deserve better
and I promise I'll believe you.

Forgiveness

Lately,
I've found myself digging deeper and deeper into my
reservoir of forgiveness.
Last time I reached so far that my fingers scraped
against rock bottom
and I was forced to collect the residual letters from
halfhearted phrases of the past.
I used them to form a less than emotionless "okay"
and slid it your way to appease your ego.
This is the norm for us...
how it became an annoying habit of me to pull
excuses,
self-blame,
pity,
and anything else from the depths of my
consciousness
just so you could remain the innocent party in our
dysfunctional relationship.
But I've come to the conclusion that...
I cannot continue to reach for exoneration that isn't
there simply because guilt has always has been your
favorite card to play in my life.

I am not guilty, you are.
And still,
I forgive you
anyway.

Coexist

We still coexist in each other's subconscious thoughts
and every now and then
around 3 am
we meet up at the glass partition dividing the past
from the present.
You tell me it still drives you crazy to reach out but
never actually reach me.

You say I've forgotten you.

There's a wall between us
but I still feel you pulling.
My heart isn't elastic but I still let you reach and pull
until it strains.
I'm standing at this glass separation again and so are
you.
It's 3:25 am and we're doing this again.
No one knows we suffer together more mornings
than not.
I feel you, I do.
I hurt too, I do...

but it's toxic.

Wobble

You wanted to be held.
So I held you to a higher standard
and the pedestal proved you unsteady.

CONGEALED

Speechless

I've run out of interesting titles for this, for us, for
you and this pain.
I was almost okay —
almost not broken
almost whole
almost complete
almost self-appreciative
almost.
Thought I was ready to jump
ready to leap out on faith
but I wasn't prepared to fall for anyone.
That was a minor detour on my road to progress
as I tried my best not get lost and wind up on Rock
Bottom Drive.
I just grazed that exit sign
because I ignored all the warning signs
along the way.
They told me I wasn't ready to love someone like
you
that my heart wasn't designed for
a quick spurt of love that would reach overdrive
before it reached its potential.
That's not your fault —
you never even knew what you were doing
or maybe you did.
Regardless,
I went pummeling into you anyway
forgetting I'm not a crash test dummy
and that this subtly beating heart of mine doesn't
come with air bags
a safety belt

or an insurance policy.
I really must be more careful with it
considering it's the only one I've got and currently,
it's just barely together.
But somehow I keep going,
even though it feels like I'm going nowhere fast.
I could just be on my way to the next destination.
What if I just stayed
to witness every part of you
no matter how foreign to this concept you may be.
I can't help that I want you
even at your worst.
They say stars shine brightest when they're
exploding.
I see a galaxy in your eyes in the midst of meltdowns
that ignites my soul and sets my heart ablaze.
I don't think you understand the ways that I
unintentionally love you.
That's why I'm so lost
mindlessly wandering down your mind's path.
It would seem that I've been lost within you for some
time.
It all started when I drove off the cliff
fell into those brown oceans you call eyes
and started drowning in the glimmers of your soul
that you allowed me to see from time to time.
It was the only emotional death I was willing to
allow that wasn't tainted in mediocrity.
And honestly, I don't know what else to say.
I guess I've run out of words and ways to explain...
this,
us,
you,
and this pain.

love, Love Backstory

Normally, my poetry is from a deeply personal perspective. This was the first time I wrote a piece that was completely observational. Every so often we witness loved ones experiencing uncomfortable events and all we can do is observe. I've learned over the years that if someone doesn't ask for your advice, you don't give it because it could result in pushing them even more into the arms of danger. It is best at times to not intervene and allow others to feel and work out their relationships for themselves. It may hurt us not to speak up but trust is also very crucial. When I wrote this, I wanted to put myself in the shoes of someone else. Empathy is necessary in order to understand why someone would stay in a situation that doesn't seem to make sense from the outside looking in. It was in writing this that I was able to find peace with a relationship that was not mine and trust that my loved one would do what was best for them.

love, Love

I love, Love.

Love...kisses me with the softest lips,
I'm always greeted by them—
Kisses to remind me how much I've been missed.
Love holds me as if I'm rare
As if Love has been searching for me,
Spending years on the hunt and now that love found me,
Love won't let go of me.
I secretly hope Love never does.

I love, Love.

Love's touch sends chills throughout my being.
I tingle just from Love's fingertips.
I shudder at Love's gaze.
I certainly hope it always feels this way.
I never thought we would end up here, in this place.
After all, Love didn't look anything like I could imagine
But soon became everything I ever wanted.
I'm convinced that Love is a chameleon.

I love, Love.

Love cooks for me
And cleans up too.
This isn't about just what Love can do.
Love holds me when I am weak.
But every so often, Love holds on too long for me.

Sometimes I just want to be free.
But I know Love just wants what's best for me.
After all, Love is constantly checking up on me.

I love, Love.

I've never had a love that was so attentive before.
I'm convinced that Love knows everything about my soul.
Love finds ways to learn about me that are unconventional.
Love is always inquiring about how to love me specifically.
It makes me feel special that Love goes through so much just to be with me.
I'd do anything for Love now.
I just know Love and I are meant to be.

I love, Love.

But sometimes, Love does get upset with me.
I'll admit that I'm not perfect
And Love feels everything so deeply.
Love accuses me of lying every once in a while.
I promise Love I'm being honest.
And Love swears I'm not really in this for the long haul.
Love always makes me feel like I'm doing something wrong.
Love tells me to get myself together or Love will be gone.

I think I love, Love.

Love constantly leaves emotionally.
Love checks out just to check back in
So I can feel Love's wrath
Of everything Love has been holding in.
Love hurts my feelings just so I can feel miserable
too.
Love threatens to leave physically,
But I don't want Love to.
So I beg Love to stay just for one more day.

I worry about Love.

I don't know what to do anymore.
I feel physically sick to my stomach
And it feels like Love is choking me.
Love's hands never actually grip my throat,
But I obsess over making Love happy.
So all my muscles get tense and make it hard to
breathe.
It seems that loving Love is too much for me.
Love is draining the very life out of me.

I tell myself that I still love, Love.

I defend Love all the time.
I tell my peers they've just never experienced a love
as deep as mine.
So Love's actions are forgivable and everything is
fine.
Then they remind me of all those other times.
But strangely in the moment,
I can only remember what went wrong with Love
this time.
I know what's best for me

Love just really loves me, they'll see...

Yes, I DO love, Love.

I just had a momentary lapse of judgement.
Love is all I've ever wanted.
I mean, yes sometimes Love is a little too jealous.
And occasionally Love makes comments just to push
my buttons.
But that's Love,
And I love, Love even if Love is sometimes a jerk.
I just want peace
Even though Love does know how to get me where it
hurts.

I just want to love, Love.

Is that so bad?
This is longest love I've ever had.
Forgive me for wanting to hold on even when it
seems crazy.
I worry that I may never be loved again
That maybe this is as good as it gets...
I don't remember being this insecure before Love and
I met?
Shouldn't I feel happier than this?
Love doesn't even try to fix it.

Is this really love, Love?

I mean maybe we should really think about this.
Is it still considered a mistake if Love keeps doing it?
And why are these actions always followed up with
gifts?

My broken heart is no longer mended by Love's kiss.
Love clenches instead of cradles.
My heart is so constricted.
I've lost my natural glow.
Love doesn't seem to care if I even smile anymore.

This love hurts, Love.

Love reminds me of something I can't put my finger on.
Maybe I fell for Love quickly because Love was just as familiar as pain.
Love clung to me because I clung just as hard driving us both insane.
Love really isn't all that bad,
But we are really bad for one another.
Let me go, Love, before we really hurt each other.
We can't keep breaking our own hearts and blaming the other.
Love, don't you understand?

I will always love you, Love.

This love is just got too intense for us.
Love wants to control.
Love tries to be bold.
Love wants so badly to hold…on.
Love tries to leave but can't.
Love lashes out but always regrets.
Love tries to be the very best.
But I know Love is tired just like me.

I love you, Love…but it's time we set each other free.

Sock & Buskin Backstory

Earlier, when I introduced you all to the piece "love, Love" I mentioned that I was observing what I deemed to be a very unhealthy relationship. I also mentioned that I couldn't understand it because I had never been in one like it to pass judgement as to why someone would stay. This piece came about as a result of experiencing my own walk with toxicity. Although the piece itself may appear to be full of metaphors and imagery, it's honestly not. To make it simple, I felt like I was an actress in a play except I wasn't acting at all. There is something very dark and sinister about people who like to control and manipulate every aspect of their own lives, including others who are a part of their lives as well. Though I am not rebellious, I will always stand up for myself and defend when necessary. When this became an issue and the mask began to fall off, I realized I was dealing with someone that was nothing like the character they portrayed at the beginning. What's worse is that I realized what its like to be emotionally abused and not even realize it is happening until the cycle has been going on long enough to leave a scar. Don't fret. The mask has been removed and I removed myself from the situation. Join me in the theater?

Sock & Buskin

Masks tend to hide everything but the eyes
windows to the soul
and souls only reside where they can thrive
but when I looked into yours eyes…
no one was home.

Your facial expression drips with charm
Sinister smile
you could never mean any harm.
Your disguise is serving its purpose.
I am now unknowingly part of your play.

You love the theatre
how people become whomever whenever.
At first,
I really fit the mold.
I am eclectic and smart,
poetic and bold,
talented in the arts
and just independent enough to spark
your interest.

Cast me into the role of leading lady
except I'm no Juliette looking for her Romeo.
No matter how often you insist
I prefer no scripts.
Let go
let me adlib.
This makes you cringe.
You just want me to stick to your script.

Key word being your.

What good are instructions in life and love?
I'm too free spirited but you love the thought of me
that's why you casted me
put me on a pedestal and groveled at my feet.
I never asked for this —
to be the star of your delusional dreams.

This is too much
but since you've placed me here,
maybe I can make a minor suggestion.
I'm more Christine of the Opera and you're my
Phantom.
This isn't some tragic love story
but it is your obsession.

I could have loved you
but you're hiding something.
Something about me triggers something in you
and pieces of your façade chip away in the blink of
an eye
along with some of your charm.
That same smile became sarcasm and condescension.
You can't help yourself but you have to save face,
I mean mask,
so you insist it's all jokes trying to console me before
I decide to leave your grasp.

Except you never fully had me to begin with.
At least not the way you wanted
so you fed me more lines
more duties
and greater expectations but only in your mind

71

then criticized me for not fulfilling a role I never
knew was mine.
You chastise me with the fact that the previous
actress performed it better
yet still you left her behind.
This feels like a game and I'm no longer inclined
to play.

So I ask...
What is this?
What am I to you?
I was everything and now I just seem to annoy you.
What did I do?
I can feel the distance and if I'm not what you want
I can leave if you'd like me to.
It's no problem.

Cut
Close curtain
End scene

This isn't part of your script.
You hate it when I veer off.
I'm not following the lines
but you're giving me all the signs
to leave.
I can tell this isn't how you expected it to go
because who could have the audacity to let you go?

You remind me you are superior
and I'm lucky to have your time.
At least that's what you tell me,

but I know you're just telling yourself.
You have to keep boosting your inner self.
Remember I can see your mask
and all it's hairline cracks.

You really don't like that.

So cold words pass your lips
and you say it with a straight face
but with little conviction.
You don't even believe it
but masks don't have expressions.
so what am I supposed to believe?
You say this is nothing to you
when we're alone
but act like we're everything when others can see.
You still need me for your imaginary play
and you manipulate me to stay.
"Relax and go with the flow,"
you say.
"You're just oversensitive. It won't always be this
way…"

You assure me that this is just a rough patch and all
great love stories have one.
except this isn't love
because now I'm being punished behind the scenes
for no reason.
You want more and more and you expect everything
while telling me you don't want anything.
I never asked for all or nothing
but I'd like to mean something.
This is all so confusing.

You don't get to write the outcome of this play
I wield the pen this time.
Retreat like you do when you're upset.
The silent treatment won't work
I'm ready to exit stage left.

When it's time for me to go
you start a monologue to a nonexistent audience
and nothing makes sense.
You want to justify hurting me just to keep me in
your presence?
I can't do this anymore.
It's really gotten ugly—
where is my understudy?

But I wouldn't wish this on her either.

Your perception of love is warped.
You can't mold me into what you want.
This isn't a play and I am real.
But since you love a good actor
someone becoming whomever whenever
Then you know that—
Romeo and Juliette loved but couldn't be together,
and the Phantom was obsessed with Christine,
so he trapped her for his own pleasure—
a lot like you and me.
Except it hurt him more to keep her than set her free.
The difference between you and the Phantom
is that you were just fine with keeping me
despite how I felt
and I'm not so sure feeling is something you do.

Your mask completely fell and I still don't know you.

I guess it's because masks can hide everything but
the eyes
the windows to the soul
and souls can only reside where they can thrive.
but every time I look into your eyes…
there's never anyone home.

Make Believe and Imaginary Things

I think about my past everyday.
I pray that those I have loved have found peace and
solace,
that my shortcomings have not left them ill
tempered.
Shell of a person
I was...
Skin just barely encasing a soul that had yet to find
its purpose.
I apologize for being subtly toxic.
Immaturity masked in a well put together package.
But the truth is,
I've always known better —
how to be better —
that I was in fact better —
than what you all received.
Forgive me
For not knowing how to give all of me
when I was receiving all of you.

Ignorance is only bliss if you allow yourself to
become complacent.

Yet I was comfortably uncomfortable —
staying just long enough to leave an impact,
and leaving before I ever got attached...
At least I tried...
I'll never understand why they all loved me...
genuinely.
My cup overflowed with their emotions,
all looking up to me

when my back wasn't strong enough to hold me up
let alone any pair of us.
Spineless creature acting as though I had a backbone.
So far from perfect that it's laughable
but somehow I've always been deemed a good thing,
a too good to be true type thing.
I'm still wondering how they found nerve to believe
in me.
Me
a walking lie with good intentions but no plan of
action.
See I'm not that bad a person,
I just never knew what I'd actually do with any one
of you...
but I cared.
I loved.
I just don't think I was worthy of the intensity.
And you all trusted me,
With your hearts
souls
minds
and bodies.
Even when I gave each of you a specific reason to ask
God for peace
constantly losing sleep
over me...
I showed you that paradise cannot reside within
people —
that honeymoon phases are really short lived.
Because you'll always yearn for home even when
you're having the time of your life...
and surprise...
I looked like home too.

A tragic contradiction how the heart can't decipher
between the two.
No matter how imaginary my actions may have
been,
how often you had to make believe that I was real...
I hate that I was once just a facade...
I've torn it all down now.
Here I stand,
completely living in my truth.
It gets exhausting when you're constantly on the
run...
Especially from the souls that could be the ones...
And for one...specifically
I apologize for giving you something to really believe
in,
for failing and ruining your image of what love is,
or maybe I showed you how ugly it can be
and still persist.

Years later and the heart strings still flutter.

Maybe,
Just maybe...
What we had wasn't imaginary at all.

Slip

Lately,
our hugs goodbye have become a reflection of our
weakening relationship.
They are frail and barely noticeable
like arthritic fingers gripping a jar...
it could easily slip away at any given time.
And we do that;
we slip away from one another because neither of us
is strong enough to hold on.
It's easier this way.
It's best not to get too attached because stay is a
foreign concept to our generation.
Maybe I'm thinking too much.
Maybe, I just want to hold on until it feels the same
again.
Maybe
I
just
want
to
hold
on.

Levels of Toxicity

Soulmates or toxic waste?
Pollution for the heart
and hazardous to the mind,
keep warning yourself of the danger label
but it's so hard to deny the attraction.
The toxicity of this love affair is potent
and having this lover around is less than satisfaction
yet having them away feels like something is lacking.
You tell yourself,
"Please stay away this time."
They have already shown their true self.
Evil blows below the belt
and constant bickering.
But one 'I love you' is supposed to suffice
for the many nights of pain.
Tears falling to help release repressed feelings to
keep you sane.

The heart never knows when to stop loving.

Hesitate

I understand
no one has ever promised to stay and meant it.
People are compiled of shortcuts and easy exits
when the terrain gets too rough.
I get it…
but I've been on the scenic route all this time,
enjoying you
every bit of you
the way you word things,
your mind
your thought process…
those eyes that tell a story before you even speak.

And for me, that's so terrifying.

Interacting with you is something like being charged
at by a locomotive.
Standing in the middle of the tracks
completely ready for the impact but not at all ready
for the impact
if that makes sense.
I wasn't ready.
I wasn't ready to accept that someone could be so
interested in me
that my thoughts or jokes could intrigue someone
like yourself.
For some reason I can make you laugh.
I thought I was the only one captivated here
but it seems that you were too.

I ruined that.

I must seem something like a coward
like the rest in your mind...
ready for an easy exit,
But I promise I'm not.
Fear paralyzed all the bravery I had before,
I pulled back from you
told you I wasn't sure
and that hurt didn't it?
It hurt to see the cycle seemingly repeating itself.
but I have been in love before
and unlike some who have been hurt
I don't run from it.
If anything
I embrace it because there's no greater feeling than to
be wanted
to feel that someone desires to be around you.
I got attached
so I silently vowed to never give up on you.
That was hard
considering I tend to have a hard time holding on to
people
and promises too.

But I've become way too comfortable with my alone.

So much so,
that the thought of entertaining another seemed
pointless...
until you stepped back from me.
I realized that my alone was sweet
but your presence was so much sweeter...
and for the first time in a quite some time,
I was hurting.

I couldn't understand why I was so deeply into my
feelings,
how someone I seemingly just met
had so much pull on the strings of my heart.
But you do
and I'm not afraid to admit that.

Everything about you
Scares me so badly.
But I tore down my barriers anyway
and I'm standing here in the middle of track
waiting for this locomotive.
I won't flinch.
I won't hesitate.

I am here.

Ricochet

Words like I and miss and you have a hard time
coming together in my throat.
They fear forming an eerie statement
that often ricochets off the walls of silence I get in
return.

I don't say I miss you anymore.

REPURPOSED

Letter To My Ex 2 Backstory

As with any relationship, we are able to reflect and realize that in hindsight, we played a part in the demise. Some years later, it became uncomfortably clear that I had some toxic flaws that contributed to our fall. I didn't go as far as presenting this new poem to my ex, but I did think it was necessary to right my wrongs if you will by way of poetry. I later found that even that was not enough to ease my discomfort so I took the next step and formally apologized. We are now on good terms and able to have healthy conversations. Every now and then, we even share a couple of laughs. When you think there has been too much pain to come back, simply taking accountability and taking the first step to apologize can take you very far. As I reflected here, I was able to acknowledge and grow but I have grown even more since then. Own your mistakes and apologize when necessary.

Letter To My Ex 2

I won't bother greeting you in this letter,
I'll just get straight to the point.
Do you ever regret loving someone who destroyed
you?

That's what someone asked me in regards to you the
other day,
and honestly,
I couldn't even bring myself to answer at the time.
So I went home and began to write.
I thought I was done writing about you a year ago
when I took that anger,
frustration,
and sadness and typed it into a 3 page single space
poem.

I thought it would be enough
just to get it out of my system.
When it wasn't,
I hit record and posted it—
then watched the comments flood in like
look how beautiful pain can be.

My broken heart was a Picasso
and I swear I never meant to make a mockery of your
love for me,
for it to become a blood stained masterpiece nailed to
the walls of their memories.
I know you saw it and I'm sorry,
but I was hurt.

No matter how hard I tried to keep those unwanted
thoughts buried away,
those feelings would still seep out and cling to my
skin
like maggots on the carcass of our dead love.
I felt so gross trying but failing to wash unrequited
love off of me back then.
So I hope you understand why I had to write you one
last time.

I spoke too much about my own feelings before,
It's time I address yours.
Love is nothing to regret in any capacity,
even if it meant you temporarily taking my heart out
of my chest
and dissecting it for your science experiment
looking for true love in the chambers and crevices
simply because you had trust issues.

And that's okay,
Don't we all?
Aren't we all a little broken by the time someone
who actually cares comes along?
You were more than broken—
you were a complex compilation of shattered glass
like skin,
A heart surrounded by porcupine needles,
and a soul that refused to touch mine at first because
of fingers that could compete with the likes of
Wolverine and Edward Scissor Hands.

But I wasn't there to break you anymore.
You couldn't figure me out,

how I could fall in love with a walking talking
paradox—
You wanted to love without limits but you were
terrified of crossing boundaries.
You couldn't fathom
How I could want to put you back together from the
millions of pieces you were in.
I walked into your life with no armor whatsoever
and pulled every single quill out of your barely
beating love organ and actually stuck around
to watch it heal.

You were my eternity puzzle
but just like any puzzle,
once the picture is complete,
you can still see the lines where all the pieces are
joined together.
Maybe I formed the complete picture,
But I couldn't make you whole…
and that's okay.
I served my purpose for you.

So to answer the question,
I will never regret you,
or us,
or how we loved like tectonic fault lines—
abrasively and just enough to shake up our two
worlds
but gently enough to remain close by
and I will always be here if you ever need me.

Maybe we met at the wrong time,
wrong place,
wrong lifetime…

But I will always love you.

Thank you for teaching me how to love
unforgivingly…
Please know that I am okay now.

I just really thought you deserved a better goodbye
than the last time.

Come Back

You've been running all your life,
never once considering the possibility.
You're different,
always feeling like you have to chase what must be
yours,
that love could never just…
present itself in front of you.
Have you ever felt worthy of
accepting love,
not just giving it?
It isn't easy once you've developed a security blanket
of what you know to be true;
never allowing yourself to be exposed to the
unknown.
I don't know your complete past,
but do I want to?
Of course.
But now is the present,
so let this strange new love exist in the present,
and don't shy away from what is now
or what could be the future.
You're letting your inhibitions get the best of you,
while I…
I don't chase,
I just wait for the realization of something beautiful.
Do you know me?
I think you should by now,
and if so,
then what are you so afraid of?
I will allow you to run away,
because sometimes,

people need to see things for themselves.
You can run until you can't run anymore.
But I promise,
I'll be waiting for you at the final destination
because you can't run away from love.

You'll always come back.

The Good Fight

Stand up for your heart
when the demons of the past come knocking
and the future lacks light.
Remind it that it's the only muscle strong enough to
give a backbone strength to be upright.

Fight for it
the same way you fight for another's validation.
It is only as strong as you are.

Breathe

I'm not as forgetful as I used to be.
When I look in the mirror now,
the reflection is more familiar than ever and I'm
getting back to myself.
I like that.
I got lost in the dismantled bits of others.
When I say others,
I mean literally everyone because no one is really
complete.
I fell in love with their brokenness.
I'm not afraid to admit that.
I love that I've never been afraid to feel or admit to
vulnerability.
After all,
life is a dead end road with no mile markers to
indicate when you could be at the end.
So I'm fearless
because I don't know if there's just some sign that
says times up or if there's a cliff—
if I'll go peacefully or battle until my last breath.
Whatever the case,
I don't want my emotions to be a cliffhanger.
They need to know how I feel.
I'm raw.
Just as raw as I can get without ripping my flesh off
to bare my soul.
All I know is that,
I don't really have life figured out yet and I stopped
stressing because it seems no one else does either.
I'm too young to be stressed
and too old to be carefree.

There is no in between.
But I've learned to just be,
to breathe.
I stopped inhaling others and exhaling myself
because I needed to breathe,
not just absorb what made everyone else comfortable
with me.
Now, my lungs are drowning in my own confidence
while I make my way back to me.

Believe

I still pray for you,
even though sometimes,
I have no idea who I'm praying to or what exactly I'm
praying for.
I guess love really is my religion because my heart
still finds salvation in the sound of your voice.
Your existence is still some godly yet unholy
experience for me and I can't do anything but drop to
my knees and pray...
for you,
for myself.
I made a sanctuary out of you and lately,
all I've felt is uncertainty .
So you don't hear from me anymore;
I wanted to believe in you but I can't seem to apply
the same method as good Christians do
with God or Jesus.
I never see you, and though I know you exist,
do you really exist for me....?

Jumpstart

To you:

Thank you for entering my life when I thought I was
numb —
When I had to use the very hands that write this now
to pump life into my soul.
Thank you for the unintentional reminder that I'm
not a love poet,
but my love organ bled beautifully when you left.
I won't regret or forget,
But I will say goodbye in the meantime.

Thank you for the jumpstart
but I can make it from here on my own.

We've Come So Far

I traveled so far
just to find solitude
within this familiar space
residing in the smile on your face.
This is what joy feels like.
You are home
where I belong
and we deserve this feeling
more than we admit.

We went so far
just to feel what we could have always felt
dealt with the unnecessary
after being tossed aside with the unmentionables.
We never had to hurt like that.
I never should have hurt you like that.

We've come so far.

Thank you for coming along on this journey with me. I hope that your soul has been well fed and trust that there will be another course, another chapter, another journey. For now, I have given myself to you and I appreciate you for making it this far.

Made in the USA
Columbia, SC
23 November 2024

47396455R00069